T0197420

Making a Difference

WRITTEN BY: JUNE WILLIAMS
ILLUSTRATIONS BY: MICHAEL MCCUE

WestBow Press books may be ordered through booksellers or by contacting:

WestBow Press
A Division of Thomas Nelson & Zondervan
1663 Liberty Drive
Bloomington, IN 47403
www.westbowpress.com
844-714-3454

Because of the dynamic nature of the Internet, any web addresses or links contained in this book may have changed since publication and may no longer be valid. The views expressed in this work are solely those of the author and do not necessarily reflect the views of the publisher, and the publisher hereby disclaims any responsibility for them.

Any people depicted in stock imagery provided by Getty Images are models, and such images are being used for illustrative purposes only.
Certain stock imagery © Getty Images.

Interior Image Credit: Michael McCue

ISBN: 978-1-6642-6357-4 (sc)
ISBN: 978-1-6642-6358-1 (hc)
ISBN: 978-1-6642-6356-7 (e)

Library of Congress Control Number: 2022906990

Print information available on the last page.

WestBow Press rev. date: 04/14/2022

WESTBOW
P R E S S*
A DIVISION OF THOMAS NELSON
& ZONDERVAN

This book is dedicated to some of the people who have had an incredible influence on my life! First, my parents, Dr. and Mrs. Robert L. Daniel, thanks for modeling the attributes of citizenship throughout your lives and showing your children what it means to be a good citizen. What a priceless gift, and one of the reasons I feel the need to share this book!

Secondly, to the members of Hosannah Dance Company, past and present, who have been some of the most inspiring citizens I have ever known! The dedication, courage and love that you have shared with audiences up and down the East Coast, and the hope you have ignited in every person who has watched you perform, has inspired each audience member (and me) to make a difference in other people's lives. Thanks to each of you for sharing your talents and your hearts. I love you!

Preface

During these past weeks of quarantine, Americans have had time to "take stock" and reexamine the values that they have traditionally held dear ~ the freedom to gather, to shop, to work outside their homes, to play and to enjoy each other's company. During this Pandemic, the shutdown of team sports, schools and social activities has given way to family time, where parents are at home caring for their children, fast food has been replaced by home cooked meals, people are conscious about hygiene and health, and money doesn't seem to make the world go around anymore. However, unemployment has skyrocketed, anger surges over the forced lockdown, and people are searching for the values they can model for their children in such an unsettled time.

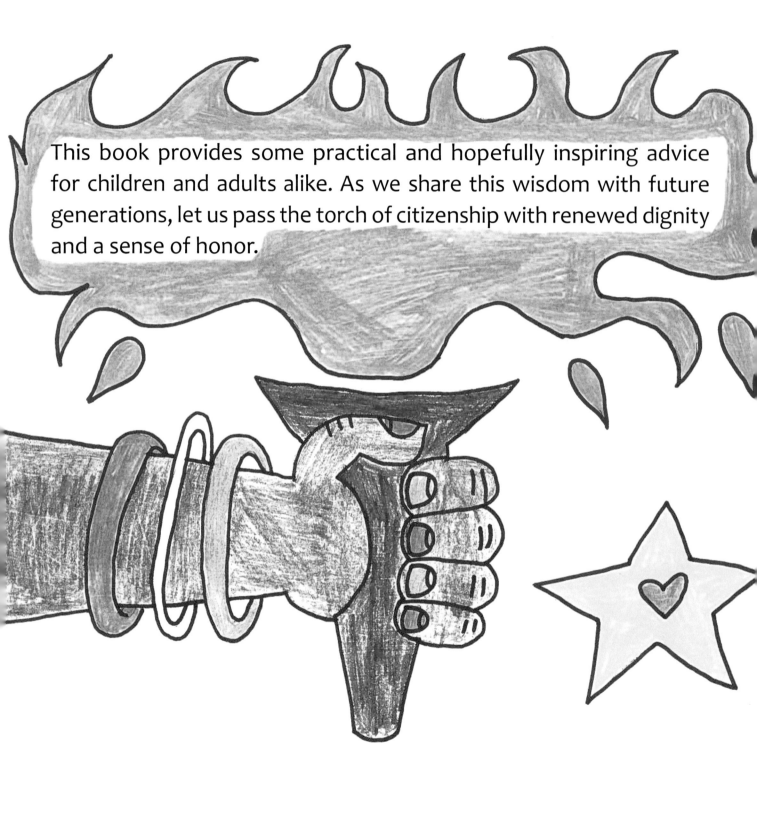

This book provides some practical and hopefully inspiring advice for children and adults alike. As we share this wisdom with future generations, let us pass the torch of citizenship with renewed dignity and a sense of honor.

Citizenship Means:

- Learning how to live peaceably with your neighbors and the environment
- Educating ourselves to meet the challenges of the 21st Century and beyond
- Understanding we are only one of the tiny specks in the Universe and more importantly, that the Universe does not revolve around us…

Being a Citizen Means:

- Learning about the history of our country and honoring the memory of those who have sacrificed greatly to make it our home.

- Acknowledging that we are only a small part of our family unit, our school society and our greater community.

- Understanding that we have responsibilities, individually and collectively, to preserve this way of life for future generations.

- In order to make a difference in this world, we need to care for our fellow human beings, love with all our hearts, and fulfill our own responsibilities in preserving our cherished way of life.

- We also need to discover our purpose~ why are we a part of this planet and what can we do to truly make a difference!!

How do we grow and develop into good citizens? First, we need to understand what it means to be a citizen. Citizenship means the honor of being a member of a certain society.

In our country, the United States of America, people can become citizens in two ways. First, when people are born in the United States, they **Automatically** become citizens, almost like being born into a family.

Second, when people come here from other countries, they can take a test, and promise to obey our laws. Then they can become **naturalized citizens** ~ similar to adoption into a family.

Being a citizen of the United States has lots of privileges. You have the right to vote, you can choose to worship or not worship, and you can attend the church of your choice, you have the freedom to speak your mind (with some limitations) and the freedom to hang out.

You also have the right to a free public education and you have the right to a jury of your peers if you have been accused of a crime.

On the other hand, being a citizen carries some responsibilities on your part. Good citizenship means obeying the laws, voting in elections so that you can make your voice heard, paying taxes and taking pride in your country and your community.

In addition to being a rule follower, good citizens also seek to make a difference in the world.

They find ways to meet the needs of others who are in poverty, they raise money for children who are sick, they volunteer their time to help animals who have not been taken care of, they visit older people who have no family and they use their time trying to make a difference in other people's lives.

Good citizens make a difference in the world because they understand that we are a community and that we all need each other.

Taking care of the vulnerable members of our society helps the people you serve, but it also helps you. When you broaden your focus to care about others, your community becomes a better place and it makes your heart happy as well.

Being a good citizen means showing kindness and understanding to each other and even choosing friends that will share that same kindness and understanding with you.

Share a listening ear with those who need you and think about things you can do that will make other people happy. In helping to create their happiness, you will ensure your own happiness as well.

When you feel anger or hurt, try to find it in your heart to forgive. Anger only hurts you and makes you sad. Try to make peace with those who have hurt you and spend your time with those friends who are positive and make you happy.

Encourage those around you as you wish to be encouraged. Support your friends and family in times of trouble; likewise, when you need support, your friends and family will be more willing to support you.

In the end, good citizenship involves the most basic truth you learned as a young child~ treating other people the same way you would like to be treated, taking care of others, and letting your conscience be your guide as you navigate your life.

As we think about how citizenship works, we must always ask ourselves ~ "What is my purpose here on earth? Am I here to just live and have a good time or is there something more for me to do?"

Your purpose, my friend, is to embrace your American citizenship and do the right thing for your fellow man. In doing that, you will always make a difference ~ and the world will be a better place because you have shared your gifts and followed your heart!

Printed in the United States
by Baker & Taylor Publisher Services